HARCOURT SCHOOL PUBLISHERS
STORYtown

READING Adventures

HOUGHTON MIFFLIN HARCOURT
School Publishers

READING Adventures

2

Teacher Read-Aloud Theme 1

Around Town

I'm Glad

I'm glad the sky is painted blue.
And earth is painted green.
With such a lot of nice fresh air
All sandwiched in between.

Anonymous

People I Know

Neighbors are people
Who live on my street.
They smile and they wave
Whenever we meet.

Friends are people
Who live near and far.
They come for a visit
By bus, plane, or car.

Families are made up
Of people like me,
With warm, happy hugs
Given so tenderly!

by Kate Arnold

The Wheels on the Bus

The wheels on the bus go
Round and round,
Round and round, round and round.
The wheels on the bus go
Round and round,
All around the town.

The horn on the bus goes
"Beep, beep, beep,
Beep, beep, beep, beep, beep, beep."
The horn on the bus goes
"Beep, beep, beep,"
All around the town.

SLOW

The people on the bus go
Up and down,
Up and down, up and down.
The people on the bus go
Up and down,
All around the town.

Traditional Song

Activity Central

A Day at the Park

You can use words to name people, animals, things, and places in the picture. Some of these words are **boy, dog, ball,** and **park.** Can you find them?

Turn and Talk

With a partner, name people, animals, things, and places in the picture. Then take turns making up sentences about them. Tell what the person, animal, or thing does.

Dog School

by Joseph Bruchac

illustrated by G. Brian Karas

Wags is my dog.
He likes to sit with me.

Wags likes to play with me.
Wags likes to sit in his tub, too.
Pop! Pop! Pop!

One day, Wags will not sit!

One day, Wags digs and digs!
I tell him he is a bad dog.
Wags is sad.

Mom tells me Wags is not bad.
Wags has to learn how to act.
He can go to dog school.

Lots of dogs go to dog school.

Wags did not do a good job
at school.

All the dogs sit and stay.
Can Wags learn to sit and stay?

Will Wags learn to sit and stay?

It is the last day of dog school.
Dogs have to sit and stay
to pass the test.

I tell Wags to sit.
Wags sits.

I tell Wags to stay.
Wags stays.

Wags did learn!
He did pass the big test!

Mom is glad.
Wags has a big kiss for me.

Wags is a good dog.
Wags is my pal!

Activity Central Picture This!

When you describe something, you use words to tell how it looks, sounds, smells, tastes, and feels. Drawing a picture or making a visual that your listeners can look at helps make your description easier to understand. Your listeners can see the details that you describe.

Choose your favorite person or animal from
Dog School. Think about the words you
would use to describe that character. Then
draw a picture, make a puppet, or make a
mask to show what the character looks like.

Turn and Talk

Describe the character to a partner. Use
what you made to help you tell what the
character is like.

What Can You See?

by Margaret K. George

illustrated by Pete Whitehead

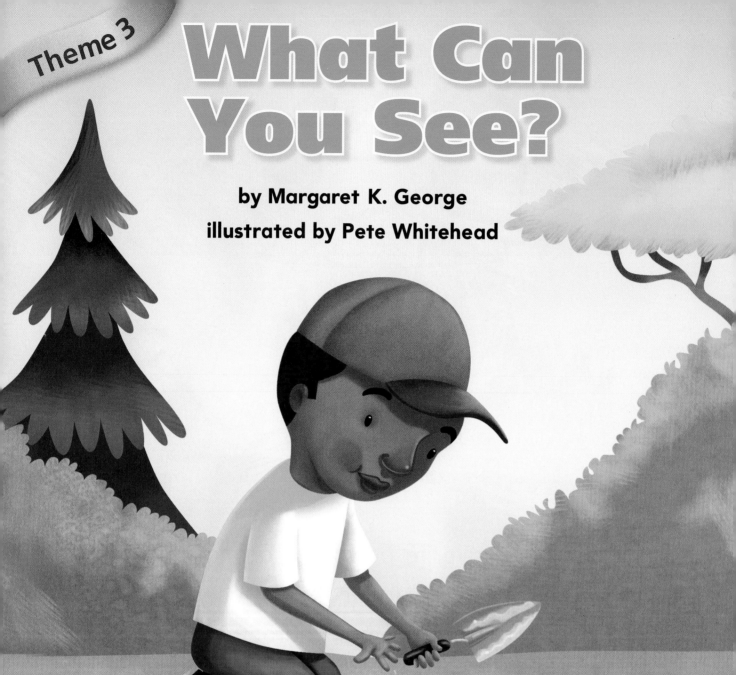

Many plants begin
as a small seed.

What can you see?
I see wet dirt.
That's all.

A small seed sprouts.
A bean plant gets big, big, big!

What can an ant see?

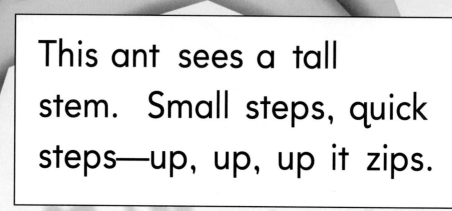

This ant sees a tall stem. Small steps, quick steps—up, up, up it zips.

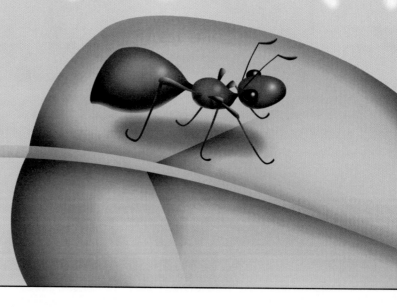

That ant runs on a leaf. A stem holds many leaves up in the fresh air. Green leaves use the sun's light to make food for the plant.

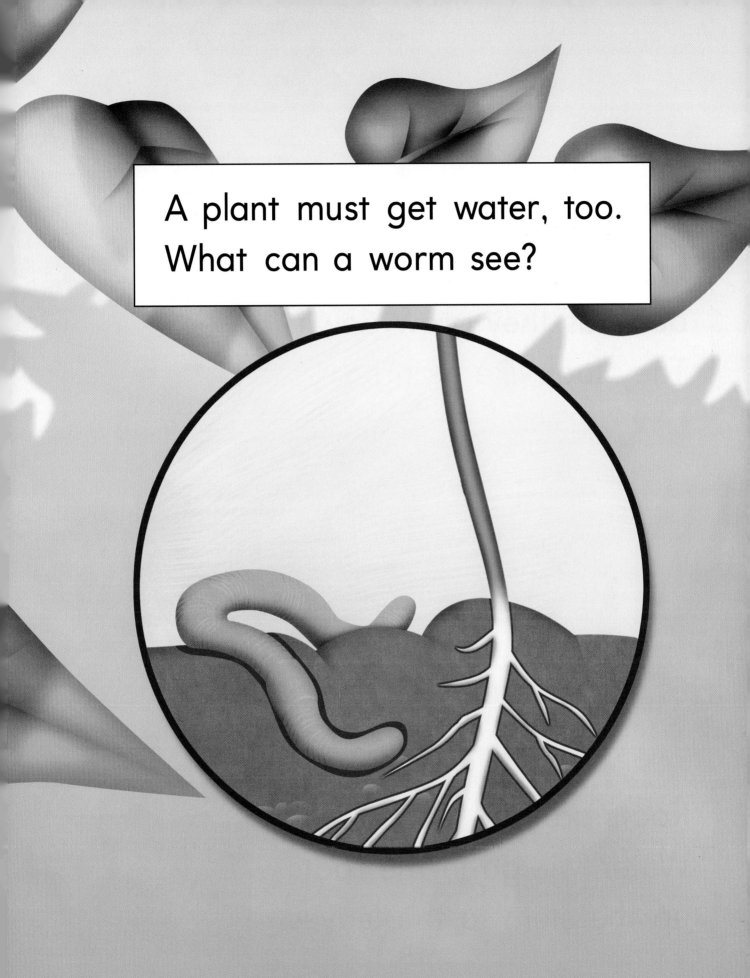

A plant must get water, too.
What can a worm see?

This worm digs by lots of thin roots. Roots twist and bend as they grow down. They look like string.

Roots are like thin straws. Water will go in the roots up the stem to the leaves.

The plant grows more and more.
What can a bee see?

This bee sees a flower. The plant has many flowers now. A small bean will grow in each flower's spot.

Now what can you see?
I see beans! Let's pick them!
What can you see in this bean?
I see seeds!

37

Word Detective

Think about each word on the next page. Is it an animal, a plant, or clothing? Make a chart like this one. Write each word where it belongs on the chart.

Animals	Plants	Clothing

Turn and Talk

When you are finished, work with a partner to think of more words to add to your chart.

flower

fox

hat

bear

grass

lamb

jacket

tree

dress

Carmen Feels Proud

by Daniel Claire   illustrated by Micha Archer

"I'm glad we're going for a walk, Dad," said Carmen. "The beach is sunny and quiet. It's not quiet in the house. Jon cried when Mom put him in the crib. When will he stop, Dad?"

"Carmen, your brother Jon is still little,"
said Dad. "Jon is not a big kid yet like you.
When you were little, you cried a lot, too."

"You are not little now, Carmen," Dad said with a grin. "Think of all the things you can do as a big girl! You can ride a bike."

"Yes! You showed me how," Carmen said.
"It was hard at first, but you helped me.
I was glad when I learned how to ride it
on my own!"

"You learned how to read, too.
Was that hard to do?" Dad asked.

"Yes, it was hard when I first started,"
Carmen said. "You and Mom helped me.
First you read stories to me. Now I can
read stories to you. I like reading!"

"I was proud of you when you learned to tie your own shoes. How did you feel?" asked Dad.

"I felt proud," Carmen said. "I can do so much on my own now. I can ride a bike, read, and tie my own shoes!"

"Jon is little," Dad said. "He can't do things
like that yet. He will need us to help him."

"I can help!" Carmen said.

"I see my cute little brother with Mom!"
Carmen called. "I'm going to give him a big
hug! Then I'll read to him and show him it is
fun. I'm glad Jon is still little!"

What Am I?

All animals change as they grow. Work with a partner to match each baby animal to a grown-up animal. Talk about how they are the same and different.

Babies

Adults

Look carefully at the pictures of the animals.
We can describe each animal in many ways.

I can describe a duck by telling what it is and what it does.

A duck is a bird.

A duck swims.

Write

Choose one of the animals and define it. Tell what kind of animal it is and how it moves.

A duck is a bird that swims.

Healthy Habits

by Judy Kentor Schmauss

You can do many things to stay healthy. Let's read about some of them. See how many of them you do!

Get exercise every day.

Exercise makes your heart and body strong. It gives you energy and helps you feel great. Play tag, swing on a swing, jump rope, or just run, run, run! Turn off the TV and exercise!

53

Get the sleep you need.

Your body needs rest each day. Your brain needs rest, too. First graders need about ten hours of sleep each night. A good night's sleep helps give you lots of energy!

Eat healthy foods.

Fruits and vegetables are fine to eat all the time. Pizza is okay to eat sometimes. Save ice cream for a special dessert. When you eat healthy, you'll feel healthy!

Foods to Eat

Eat **More** of These Foods	Eat **Less** of These Foods

Let's Move!

by Sam Wallis

Exercise makes your body strong. It is good for your bones, muscles, lungs, and heart. When you exercise, your heart pumps blood to all parts of your body. When your heart works hard, it gets stronger. A strong heart is important for a healthy body.

Many things you do each day are exercise. Do you walk to school? That's exercise! Do you play with your dog? That's exercise, too. When you make your muscles work, your heart pump, and your breathing speed up, that's exercise!

Here are good ways to get exercise. Try them all! Which ones do you like best?

- Jump rope.

- Ride a bike.

- Go for a walk.

- Go for a swim.

How will you get exercise today?

Statue

Playing **Statue** is a fun way to exercise.

How to play:

1. Get at least three friends.

2. Pick a person to be IT. That person says "Go!"

3. The players who are not IT move in funny ways. They can wiggle, spin, march, or hop.

4. The person who is IT yells "STATUE!"

5. All players freeze like a statue.

6. The player who moves first will be IT.

This game will make you laugh. Did you know that laughing is good for you, too?

Activity Central

Word Power!

Some words mean almost the same thing. Read the words below. Each word tells how someone moves. How is the meaning of each word a little bit different?

walk

skip

run

Now read these words. Each word tells about the size of something. How is the meaning of each word different?

big　　　　**huge**　　　　**gigantic**

Take turns with a partner. Choose a word from the boxes below, and act it out. Your partner will say which word it is and tell what it means.

look	**peek**	**glare**

pleased	**excited**	**happy**

The Heroes Behind the Heroes

by Sheila Sweeny

Jesse Owens **and** Charles Riley

When Jesse Owens was little, he loved to run. He ran to school. He ran back home. He was not the best runner then. When he grew up, he became one of the best runners of all time. He did it with help from his coach, Charles Riley.

Charles Riley was a
teacher at Jesse's school. He
also coached the track team.
Coach Riley loved teaching
his students how to run
faster. He was happy when
his students did their best.
He showed them how to
be winners.

One day, Coach Riley saw Jesse Owens run. He saw that Jesse was eager to win. He knew that Jesse could be a great runner. He wanted to help him run faster. He asked Jesse to join the track team.

Coach Riley showed Jesse the best way to run. He told him to step lightly on the ground with his feet. He told Jesse to pretend the ground was on fire when he ran. They practiced every day. Soon Jesse was the fastest runner in the school.

Coach Riley told Jesse to always do his best. Jesse did his best. He broke a world record when he was still in high school! Later, Jesse went to the Olympics. He won four gold medals. He became a hero all over the world!

Jesse Owens never forgot
how much Coach Riley helped
him. Jesse Owens loved to run.
Coach Riley loved to teach.
They were both very good at
what they did.

Temple Grandin (and) William Carlock

Dr. Temple Grandin is a scientist and a teacher. She studies animals and writes books about them. She helps people understand why animals act the way they do. Temple shows people how to take good care of animals.

Temple Grandin talks with a farmer.

Temple writes about how animals think, act, and feel.

When Temple was little, school was not easy for her. Temple has autism. People with autism sometimes have trouble speaking and learning. Some teachers did not know how to help Temple learn.

William Carlock was a teacher at Temple's school. He saw that Temple was smart and had talent. He helped her learn.

Temple liked science. Mr. Carlock helped her do experiments. He asked her to solve problems. He showed Temple how to think like a scientist.

This is where Temple went to school.

William Carlock helped Temple. She worked hard in school. Now she is a well-known scientist and a teacher. She teaches people about autism and about animals. Temple is a hero to people and animals all around the world!

Activity Central

On the Right Track!

A **menu** helps you find information on a website.

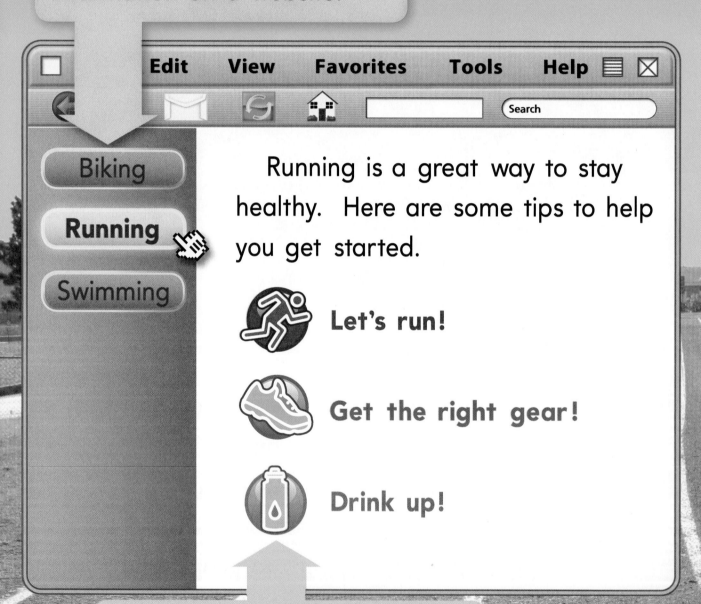

Edit   View   Favorites   Tools   Help

Search

Biking

Running

Swimming

Running is a great way to stay healthy. Here are some tips to help you get started.

Let's run!

Get the right gear!

Drink up!

Icons may be pictures that show information at a glance.

Use the website to answer these questions with a partner.

➤ Which icon would you click on to learn about running shoes?

➤ Which part of the menu would you click on to learn about swimming?

➤ What do you think you will find if you click on the **Drink up!** icon?

Work with your partner to think of two more icons you could add to this website. Draw your icons and add a label for each one.

Photography Credits: